# STATIONS of
# the **Infancy**

# STATIONS *of*
## the **Infancy**

Denis McBride C.Ss.R.

**redemptorist**
p u b l i c a t i o n s

Published by Redemptorist Publications
Wolf's Lane, Chawton, Hampshire, GU34 3HQ, UK
Tel. +44 (0)1420 88222, Fax. +44 (0)1420 88805
Email rp@rpbooks.co.uk, www.rpbooks.co.uk

A registered charity limited by guarantee
Registered in England 03261721

First published October 2019
Edited by Peter Edwards
Designed by Eliana Thompson

ISBN 978-0-85231-559-0

The publisher gratefully acknowledges permission to use the following copyright material:
Excerpts from The Jerusalem Bible, copyright © 1966 by Darton, Longman & Todd, Ltd and Doubleday, a division of Random House, Inc. Reprinted by permission.

Cover image: © José Luiz Bernardes Ribeiro, CC BY-SA 4.0, https://commons.wikimedia.org; pp. 71/72 Flight into Egypt I, 1979, Lawson, Gillian (Contemporary Artist) / Private Collection / Bridgeman Images. Used by permission.

Printed by Bishops Printers,
Portsmouth, PO6 1TR

# Contents

# Introduction

Two saintly men, untethered in history, believed the same thing: that the most distinguishing belief of the Catholic Church was not the resurrection but the incarnation – that the Son of the almighty God had become fully human, that the Word that was at home in God pitched his tent among us and made a new home, as the son of Mary of Nazareth, in the world of first-century Palestine. Divine majesty not only looked down, but came down to make his home among us. He was the stranger from heaven, unrecognised by his creation, unacknowledged by his own people. Hosanna, now, not in the highest but in the lowest. The two great advocates of this fundamental characteristic of Catholic belief were St Alphonsus Liguori, the founder of the Redemptorists, and St John Henry Newman, the distinguished Oratorian and theologian.

Their celebration of the incarnation was not a holy memory of an astounding event that happened two thousand years ago, but a profound appreciation of the ongoing presence of Christ in word and in sacrament and in the midst of everyday life. As Jesus taught us:

> For I was hungry and you gave me food; I was thirsty and you gave me drink; I was a stranger and you made me welcome; naked and you clothed me, sick and you visited me, in prison and you came to see me. (Matthew 25:35-36)

At the centre of Jesus' great teaching on the last judgement is the revelation that one way Jesus elects to be present to humanity is through the cry of the needy ones. His "I" is hidden in what might be regarded as a most unlikely sanctuary. Imagine for a moment three alien travellers journeying from outer space aboard their starship: they are coming with the express intention of finding an unusual king who is rumoured to be living among us. The three pilgrims land unannounced on our doorstep, carrying the gifts they have brought from afar, and tell us why they have journeyed to this place: they are looking for Jesus. We cannot help but notice their curious gifts and wonder what possible use anyone could find for them, but we say nothing. Their question brings us back to their purpose: "Where", they ask, "can we find him?"

What directions would we give? We might direct them to the church, in the hope that the priests might introduce them to word and sacrament. Or we might direct them to strange sanctuaries, such as refugee camps and hospitals and prisons, and say that Jesus himself said that he was to be found among the inhabitants there.

In the apocalyptic vision of the last judgement given to the disciples prior to his death, Jesus focuses attention on his continuing presence among those in need. It is as if Jesus deliberately turns his own followers away from an exclusive attraction to himself, away from a restricted focus on his own person, to look elsewhere to find him. In so doing, he challenges us to face the pain and loss endured by others, not keep staring at him. He will be found where others suffer – those St Alphonsus referred to as "the most abandoned". The presence of Christ continues in our midst. The incarnation is embodied in the continuing human story.

This book, *Stations of the Infancy*, celebrates the human beginning of that great adventure of God becoming human. As well as writing *Stations of the Cross*, St Alphonsus wrote the less well-known *Stations of the Infant Jesus* – twelve in all. He begins with the incarnation:

## STATION ONE The Son of God becomes an Infant.

O Jesus, born of Virgin bright, immortal glory be to Thee; praise to the Father infinite, and Holy Ghost eternally.

### Consideration
Consider that the Son of God, the Infinite Majesty, the Creator of the world, and who has need of no one, became incarnate to save lost man by his sufferings, and was for nine months enclosed as a little Infant in the most chaste womb of Mary.

### Affections
O most amiable Infant Jesus, God and Man, it was Thy burning love for me which urged Thee do, do all this. I give Thee thanks; and I beseech Thee, by Thy Incarnation, to give me the grace to correspond to such great goodness.[1]

---

1   A. Liguori, *The Incarnation, Birth and Infancy of Jesus Christ*, Ascetical Works Volume IV (New York: Benziger Brothers, 1887), 334.

I have not included St Alphonsus' wonderfully imaginative Stations, such as "Jesus is suckled"; "Jesus with his hands free from swaddling clothes"; "Jesus begins to walk"; "Jesus sleeps". While I have chosen the same beginning in the incarnation, I have concentrated on key scriptural events from the Gospels, where I feel on safer ground. I do not have my beloved founder's extraordinary sympathetic imagination to insert himself into the unknowable moments of Jesus' childhood development – all the time addressing the infant Jesus in the most affectionate terms. Although a doctor of the Church, St Alphonsus is always passionately personal about his belief, forever engaged in intimate conversation with his Lord.

Reading St Alphonsus' *Stations of the Infant Jesus* is like overhearing a loving and attentive grandfather whisper tender assurances into the cradle in the quiet of the night. His conversational intimacy and his muscular sentimentality might appear strange in a world of propriety that edges towards detachment. You feel privileged, if somewhat uneasy, to witness such overflowing devotion. You wonder about how both are so tethered together.

I have also extended the journey to fourteen Stations, to fit into the pattern of Redemptorist Publications' two other recent books *Stations of the Cross: then and now* and *Stations of the Resurrection*, making this a devotional trilogy of the birth, death and resurrection of Jesus.

I hope you enjoy journeying through the Gospel beginnings of the Jesus story, celebrating the astounding truth that God came among us in Christ at a particular time and place in history, but never forgetting that Christ comes to us every day in word and sacrament and people.

*Denis McBride cssr*

**Denis McBride C.Ss.R.**
Publishing Director

# THE FIRST STATION

The Word
Becomes Flesh

*The earth from space*

The evangelist John introduces the Word as the creator, the ancestor of all that lives, and a light that shines in the darkness. Two negative notes are sounded: when the Word comes into the world, the world does not know him; neither do his own people accept him. The Word is the stranger from heaven. To all who accept him he gives power to become children of God.

# Opening Response

In the name of the Father and of the Son and of the Holy Spirit.
**Amen.**

I believe in one Lord Jesus Christ,
the Only Begotten Son of God,
born of the Father before all ages.
**God from God, Light from Light,**
**true God from true God.**

## *Reading*

John 1:1-5. 14

In the beginning was the Word:
and the Word was with God
and the Word was God.
He was with God in the beginning.
Through him all things came to be,
not one thing had its being but through him.
All that came to be had life in him
and that light was the light of men,
a light that shines in the dark,
a light that darkness could not overpower…

The Word was made flesh,
he lived among us,
and we saw his glory,
the glory that is his as the only Son of the Father,
full of grace and truth.

# Reflection

When the evangelist John celebrates the beginning of the Jesus story he goes back before time, before history, before creation. The Jesus story in John's Gospel begins not with an adult Jesus by the River Jordan (Mark), or a newborn baby in Joseph's home in Bethlehem (Matthew), or a newborn lying in a borrowed manger in Bethlehem (Luke), but before the creation of the world. John's Messiah does not come from Bethlehem but from outside the realm of creation; neither can he be accurately identified as Jesus of Nazareth because he does not come from there but from the upper realm.

For John, the details of Jesus' earthly beginnings are irrelevant – no birth story is told, no mother is introduced, no time is recorded, no place is noted, no witnesses are named – because his true origin is beyond the cosmos: "In the beginning was the Word: and the Word was with God and the Word was God." John goes back beyond the prophetic story of Israel (Mark), and the Jewish story (Matthew), and the human story (Luke) to rework Genesis and anchor the beginning of the Jesus story in the originality of God.

Independently of the earlier three Gospels, John moves out of any historical frame and offers eternity as the real setting of the Jesus story. There is a sense in which John breaks free of any controls and limitations to the Jesus story, passes effortlessly beyond all earthly and historical barriers, to root the Jesus story in the eternity of God – a theological perception that dominates the creeds of the Church. John provides a unique interpretative backdrop against which everything he says about Jesus must be read in the light of the opening verse.

What about our origins? In the opening of the letter to the Ephesians our true origins are celebrated:

> Blessed be God the Father of our Lord Jesus Christ,
> who has blessed us with all the spiritual blessings of heaven in Christ.
> Before the world was made, he chose us, chose us in Christ,
> to be holy and spotless, and to live through love in his presence.

Ephesians 1:3-4

## *Prayer*

Most merciful God, you so loved the world
that you gave your only begotten Son,
so that whoever believes in him
may not perish but enjoy everlasting life.
Increase our faith, we pray,
so that rooted and grounded
in the mystery of the Word made flesh,
we may forever attach ourselves to the one
who is the Way, the Truth and the Life.
We ask this through the merits of the same Christ,
who lives and reigns with you in the unity of the Holy Spirit,
world without end.

**Amen.**

## Closing Response

Glory to God in the highest,
and on earth peace to people of good will.
**For you alone are the Holy One,
you alone are the Lord,
you alone are the Most High,
Jesus Christ,
with the Holy Spirit,
in the glory of God the Father.
Amen.**

# THE SECOND STATION

## The Annunciation to Zechariah

*The Annunciation to Zacharias,* **Domenico Ghirlandaio, 1486–1490**

This fresco is part of the series Ghirlandaio made for the Tornabuoni family chapel in the church of Santa Maria Novella in Florence. Ghirlandaio turned the Jewish temple into a typical Renaissance church. We see the priest Zechariah interrupted while he dutifully incenses the altar of sacrifice. The angel comes to announce the coming birth of his son John. The painter illustrates lavishly Luke's line: "the whole congregation was outside" – in this case members of the Florence government and the Tornabuoni family.

# Opening Response

In the name of the Father and of the Son and of the Holy Spirit.
**Amen.**

"Zechariah, do not be afraid, your prayer has been heard.
**Your wife Elizabeth is to bear you a son
and you must name him John."**

## *Reading*

Luke 1:5-17

In the days of King Herod of Judaea there lived a priest called Zechariah who belonged to the Abijah section of the priesthood, and he had a wife, Elizabeth by name, who was a descendant of Aaron. Both were worthy in the sight of God, and scrupulously observed all the commandments and observances of the Lord. But they were childless: Elizabeth was barren and they were both getting on in years.

Now it was the turn of Zechariah's section to serve, and he was exercising his priestly office before God when it fell to him by lot, as the ritual custom was, to enter the Lord's sanctuary and burn incense there. And at the hour of incense the whole congregation was outside, praying.

Then there appeared to him the angel of the Lord, standing on the right of the altar of incense. The sight disturbed Zechariah and he was overcome with fear. But the angel said to him, "Zechariah, do not be afraid, your prayer has been heard. Your wife Elizabeth is to bear you a son and you must name him John. He will be your joy and delight and many will rejoice at his birth, for he will be great in the sight of the Lord; he must drink no wine, no strong drink. Even from his mother's womb he will be filled with the Holy Spirit, and he will bring back many of the sons of Israel to the Lord their God. With the spirit and power of Elijah, he will go before him to turn the hearts of fathers towards their children and the disobedient back to the wisdom that the virtuous have, preparing for the Lord a people fit for him."

13

# Reflection

To understand the beginning of the story of the adult Jesus, the four Gospels point us to someone else, the figure of John the Baptist. John the Baptist is the independent prophetic force that stands between the hidden life of Jesus and his public ministry. Jesus does not begin alone; none of us does. Jesus, like many other people, is attracted by the person and preaching of John the Baptist; like many of his contemporaries, he submits to John's baptism of repentance for the forgiveness of sins. After his association with John, Jesus' life takes a dramatic turn. He follows John in the prophetic vocation and reinterprets the message of his mentor.

There is a firm anchor point in the Gospels: if you are going to tell the story of Jesus you must first tell the story of John the Baptist. This is underlined in the infancy narrative of Luke's Gospel: before the evangelist introduces us to the parents of Jesus, telling us of the annunciation of the birth of Jesus, his birth and circumcision, he first introduces the parents of John the Baptist, telling of the annunciation of the birth of John, his birth and circumcision. The tradition is firm: Jesus comes after John.

The angel Gabriel tells Zechariah of the joy and gladness which the birth of John will bring to many - not just his parents - and outlines the future career of John. John will lead a movement of conversion to God and prepare the people for the coming of the Lord. His mission is clear - to prepare for the Lord a people fit for him.

In Luke's understanding John the Baptist is the last prophet of the Old Testament: "Up to the time of John it was the Law and the Prophets; since then, the kingdom of God has been preached" (Luke 16:16). The child who is born of ancient parents will close the Old Testament; Jesus, born of the young Virgin Mary, will open the New Testament. In these two figures the unity of the whole biblical story is linked.

## Prayer

Almighty God,
who sent your servant John the Baptist
to be a herald of the coming kingdom
and to prepare a way for your beloved Son:
we pray that you might continue to call
men and women from every race and nation
to be, like John the Baptist,
a witness to speak for the light
so that people might believe in him
through the integrity of their life
and the power of their example.
This we pray in the name of Jesus, your Son.
**Amen.**

## Closing Response

Behold the Lamb of God.
**Behold him who takes away the sins of the world;
have mercy upon us all.
Amen.**

# THE THIRD STATION

# The Annunciation
## to Mary

*Virgin Annunciate,* **Antonello da Messina, 1476**

In paintings of the annunciation you usually see the angel Gabriel visiting Mary with God's message. Antonello focuses on Mary alone as she is interrupted during her reading. She is neither crowned nor does she have a halo: she is a young woman of Nazareth. In this painting we, not Gabriel, are the viewer. Each of us is invited to look at Mary, without Gabriel and without the distraction of a background, as she graciously responds to God's word.

# Opening Response

In the name of the Father and of the Son and of the Holy Spirit.
**Amen.**

Rejoice, so highly favoured! The Lord is with you.
**Let what you have said be done to me.**

# *Reading*

Luke 1:26-38

The angel Gabriel was sent by God to a town in Galilee called Nazareth, to a virgin betrothed to a man named Joseph, of the House of David; and the virgin's name was Mary. He went in and said to her, "Rejoice, so highly favoured! The Lord is with you." She was deeply disturbed by these words and asked herself what this greeting could mean, but the angel said to her, "Mary, do not be afraid; you have won God's favour. Listen! You are to conceive and bear a son, and you must name him Jesus. He will be great and will be called Son of the Most High. The Lord God will give him the throne of his ancestor David; he will rule over the House of Jacob for ever and his reign will have no end." Mary said to the angel, "But how can this come about, since I am a virgin?" "The Holy Spirit will come upon you" the angel answered "and the power of the Most High will cover you with its shadow. And so the child will be holy and will be called Son of God. Know this too: your kinswoman Elizabeth has, in her old age, herself conceived a son, and she whom people called barren is now in her sixth month, for nothing is impossible to God." "I am the handmaid of the Lord," said Mary "let what you have said be done to me." And the angel left her.

# Reflection

Mary gives the classic response of the disciple when challenged by the word of God: "Let what you have said be done to me." That is her annunciation, her consent to hand over her body and spirit to God's purpose. The love that offers itself is the love that must wait. That is why there are two annunciations: God's annunciation to Mary and Mary's annunciation to God. God's best plans can only happen when there is human cooperation, when God's word and our word come together. When those two annunciations come together, God's word always becomes flesh.

Mary, like all mothers, gives over her body and mind and soul so that new life may be born. She does this so that a life larger than hers may take its own place in the world. All mothers must wait for the gradual process that is happening within them; they must learn to let go of the child within them. They must not only nurture the presence of the child within them; they must nurture the leaving of the child. The act of childbirth is the painful act of letting go, so that the life within can take its own separate place in the world. Mary's vocation is not only to hold Jesus within her but to let him go, let him become the person he must become.

Whatever Mary was planning for her life with Joseph, it did not include becoming pregnant outside that relationship. An unexpected word interrupts the routine of life and proposes a groundbreaking diversion from what is planned; nothing less than a startling new future is proposed. Mary gives up her own wishes in order to adopt God's desire; she gives up personal control of her life in favour of God's promise; in her response she pledges her body and spirit to the purposes of God.

Mary assists the struggle of God to be one like us. There is something dangerously new about Mary. She is the woman at the centre of the Christian story. It is a woman, not a man, who brings God's real presence into the world. Through her the presence of the *Christos Kyrios* will be known and celebrated.

## Prayer

Remember, O most gracious Virgin Mary,
that never was it known
that anyone who fled to thy protection,
implored thy help or sought thy intercession,
was left unaided.
Inspired by this confidence, I fly unto thee,
O Virgin of virgins, my Mother;
to thee do I come, before thee I stand,
sinful and sorrowful;
O Mother of the Word Incarnate, despise not my petitions,
but in thy mercy hear and answer me.
**Amen.**

## Closing Response

Hail Mary, full of grace,
the Lord is with thee.
Blessed art thou among women,
and blessed is the fruit of thy womb, Jesus.

**Holy Mary, Mother of God,
pray for us sinners,
now and at the hour of our death.
Amen.**

# THE FOURTH STATION

# The Visitation:
## Mary Visits Elizabeth

**The Visitation, modern sculpture, Padre Andrea Martini OFM**

The modern sculpture of Mary and Elizabeth stands outside the Church of the Visitation in Ein Karem, Jerusalem, the traditional site of the house of Zechariah. Looking at the sculpture you notice that as the two mothers' eyes meet, their two wombs almost touch as two worlds come together. As John O'Donohue wrote in his poem "The Visitation":

Two women locked in a story of birth.
Each mirrors the secret the other heard.[1]

---

1   John O'Donohue, "The Visitation", in *Conamara Blues* (London: Doubleday, 2000), 46.

# Opening Response

In the name of the Father and of the Son and of the Holy Spirit.
**Amen.**

My soul magnifies the Lord.
**And my spirit exults in God my saviour.**

## *Reading*

Luke 1:39-45

Mary set out at that time and went as quickly as she could to a town in the hill country of Judah. She went into Zechariah's house and greeted Elizabeth. Now as soon as Elizabeth heard Mary's greeting, the child leapt in her womb and Elizabeth was filled with the Holy Spirit. She gave a loud cry and said, "Of all women you are the most blessed, and blessed is the fruit of your womb. Why should I be honoured with a visit from the mother of my Lord? For the moment your greeting reached my ears, the child in my womb leapt for joy. Yes, blessed is she who believed that the promise made her by the Lord would be fulfilled."

# Reflection

The visitation is principally a story of two women, two mothers: the young mother of Jesus and the ancient mother of John the Baptist. Their sons are important, but the visitation is not their story. In this narrative the men are secondary; Luke celebrates the mothers, the ones who carry greatness within them. However important the men will become, however heroic their lives, they will start life as we all did – waiting in the womb of our mother. Unlike the other evangelists, Luke celebrates the role of women in the birth of greatness. All greatness has the same beginnings: it starts in utter dependence on women. Luke celebrates the simple truth that all our lives are a gift from others: who we are is what we owe to others.

For Luke, Elizabeth and Mary are not just individual characters: they represent the whole of scripture. Elizabeth comes out of the Old Testament, an old woman who has waited on the promises of God. It's not just that her time has come; the final time has now arrived in the last of the prophets, her son John the Baptist. He will go before Jesus in birth, he will go before Jesus in life, and he will go before Jesus in death.

Mary, on the other hand, represents what is utterly new and fresh and startling: she is the young maiden, surprised by God. She represents the new Israel, the fulfilment of all the ancient promises, for out of her womb will come the saviour of Israel and of all humanity. She makes a journey to meet old Israel. The New Testament crosses the divide and journeys into the Old. Can the Old Testament and the New Testament recognise one another?

The old and the new come together in the recognition and greeting of Elizabeth and Mary. As soon as Elizabeth hears Mary's greeting, the old woman experiences a dance in the womb as John leaps for joy. The new time begins with womb-shaking rejoicing. Elizabeth greets Mary as "the mother of my Lord". The two women share the same Lord.

# *Prayer*

Eternal God, who looked with favour on your servant Mary
and called her to be the mother of your Son:
we ask you to nurture within in us the humility and gentleness
that found favour in your sight,
that with her we may proclaim the greatness of your name
and find the mercy you show to those who fear you;
through Jesus Christ our Lord,
who lives and reigns with you and the Holy Spirit,
one God, now and for ever.
**Amen.**

# Closing Response

The Almighty has done great things for me.
**Holy is his name,
and his mercy reaches from age to age.
Amen.**

# THE FIFTH STATION

## The Magnificat

*Madonna of the Magnificat,* **Sandro Botticelli, early 1480s**

The *Madonna of the Magnificat* is a tondo, a painting of circular form, now in the Uffizi Gallery. It celebrates the fulfilment of the Magnificat. The Virgin Mary, crowned by two angels, is writing the opening lines of the Magnificat on the right-hand page of a book which is held open by two angels. Her son's right hand guides her writing, while his left hand takes the pomegranate, a symbol of the passion, from his mother's left hand.

# Opening Response

In the name of the Father and of the Son and of the Holy Spirit.
**Amen.**

Mary said, "My soul proclaims the greatness of the Lord
and my spirit exults in God my saviour;
**because he has looked upon his lowly handmaid."**

# *Reading*

Luke 1:46-55

Mary said:

"My soul proclaims the greatness of the Lord
and my spirit exults in God my saviour;
because he has looked upon his lowly handmaid.
Yes, from this day forward all generations will call me blessed,
for the Almighty has done great things for me.
Holy is his name,
and his mercy reaches from age to age for those who fear him.
He has shown the power of his arm,
he has routed the proud of heart.
He has pulled down princes from their thrones and exalted the lowly.
The hungry he has filled with good things, the rich sent empty away.
He has come to the help of Israel his servant, mindful of his mercy
- according to the promise he made to our ancestors -
of his mercy to Abraham and to his descendants for ever."

# Reflection

Mary gives every Christian hope in the growing struggle of everyday life. In the Magnificat Luke portrays her as the one who glorifies God because "the Almighty has done great things for me". She is a woman of the people whose song delights in God's choice of her, whose spirit soars because God has not overlooked this lowly handmaid. But she is also a dangerous woman because she is the one who voices the subversive hope of the poor people and the little ones:

> He has pulled down princes from their thrones and exalted the lowly.
> The hungry he has filled with good things, the rich sent empty away.

In the Magnificat we see Mary as the radical woman. She is the woman who hungers for a new justice on earth, one that reflects the justice of God. The God who did not overlook her is the God who dethrones the mighty and exalts the lowly. In this dispensation the hungry are filled with good things, the rich sent empty away. Mary voices a contrary wisdom. She voices a radical protest against what we all take for granted: that the mighty will always prevail over the weak, that the well-fed nations will thrive while others starve to death, that the politically strong will always occupy the thrones of power.

Mary voices God's opposition to tyranny, God's determination to pull down the powers that brutalise their subjects. In that, Mary is no passive, silent woman. It is hardly surprising, therefore, that it is poor people who look to her most for help. It is them we see on our television screens carrying her statue with great dignity as they process and protest in circles outside palaces and prisons and army headquarters.

Clearly they believe something that most of us have come to forget.

# *Prayer*

Almighty God,
we pray for the Church which has Mary as mother:
that it will always proclaim your greatness
and faithfully preach the message of Christ Jesus.
We pray for all mothers:
that you will bless them and the fruit of their womb.
For poor people and for all who are persecuted:
that you will again show the power of your arm
and bring down the powers that tyrannise
your people who hunger for what is right.

We pray for the multitudes of refugees throughout the world:
that you will save them from despair and bitterness of Spirit,
and bless those who struggle for their relief and security.
This we pray through Christ our Lord.
**Amen.**

# Closing Response

The Almighty has done great things for me.
Holy is his name.
**And his mercy reaches from age to age**
**for those who fear him.**
**Amen.**

# THE SIXTH STATION

# The Birth of
# John the Baptist

*The Birth of John the Baptist,* **Giovanni di Paolo, 1454**

John the Baptist, who will be celebrated for cleansing people in the waters of the River Jordan, is now washed by a midwife with water from a bowl on the floor. The child looks at his father, Zechariah, who is seated while he writes on the scroll the message he received from the angel: "He shall be called John." In this warm domestic scene Elizabeth rests in her grand bed, pondering recent events, while a female relative dries a towel before the open fire.

# Opening Response

In the name of the Father and of the Son and of the Holy Spirit.
**Amen.**

All those who heard of it treasured it in their hearts.
**"What will this child turn out to be?" they wondered.**

# *Reading*

Luke 1:57-66

The time came for Elizabeth to have her child, and she gave birth to a son; and when her neighbours and relations heard that the Lord had shown her so great a kindness, they shared her joy.

Now on the eighth day they came to circumcise the child; they were going to call him Zechariah after his father, but his mother spoke up. "No," she said "he is to be called John." They said to her, "But no one in your family has that name", and made signs to his father to find out what he wanted him called. The father asked for a writing-tablet and wrote, "His name is John". And they were all astonished. At that instant his power of speech returned and he spoke and praised God. All their neighbours were filled with awe and the whole affair was talked about throughout the hill country of Judaea. All those who heard of it treasured it in their hearts. "What will this child turn out to be?" they wondered. And indeed the hand of the Lord was with him.

# Reflection

In the Gospel reading the family rejoices at the birth of John the Baptist and the neighbours are thrilled that the two ancients have a child at last. Everyone hovers and whispers and wonders. A question is on everyone's lips: "What will this child turn out to be?" This is a question pondered by all parents when they look adoringly into the eyes of their newborn child: "Who will our child turn out to be?"

When John the Baptist emerges as an adult prophet, he is not a man who has invented himself out of thin air. He is the product of two particular parents, a particular home, a particular background and a particular love. Like us all, much of who he has become in life he owes to others.

Like all our childhoods, John's childhood is measured by the person he becomes in later life:

- In adulthood he emerges as a man of unique authority, an independent prophet who can dominate the wilderness and attract people to come out to the wilds to listen to his message.

- He can openly confront the religious hierarchy of his day and dismiss them in one line as a brood of poisonous snakes.

- He has the charismatic personality to attract the outsiders, the fringe people, like mercenary soldiers and prostitutes and tax collectors, and offer them something institutional religion can never offer them – real hope.

- He has the unique characteristic of being the only single religious leader to attract Jesus of Nazareth; his reputation draws Jesus to his wilderness outpost. While Jesus is with John he changes his way of life in Nazareth to live as a wandering prophet and teacher.

We celebrate the birth of John the Baptist because of who John became in his later life. The significance of the adult John is pressed back into the story of his birth, a story appropriate to the measure of this great man. If the adult John the Baptist had played no significant part in the life of Jesus, the Gospel of Luke would not have celebrated his birth. We hallow the birth of John the Baptist because of the man he became for Jesus.

## Prayer

O God our loving Father,
who has crowned the love of Zechariah and Elizabeth
with the gift of their child, John,
the one who would prepare a way for the Lord
and call all people to a change of life:
grant that as we rejoice in John's birth
we may attend the challenge of his message
and his humility before the person of Jesus.
This we pray in the name of Christ our Lord.
**Amen.**

## Closing Response

And you, little child,
you shall be called Prophet of the Most High,
**for you will go before the Lord
to prepare the way for him.
Amen.**

# THE SEVENTH STATION

## Joseph
## the Dreamer

*The Dream of St Joseph*, **Georges de La Tour, 1640**

A profound silence permeates the room. There are no background scenes to distract the eye from this personal encounter between the angel and Joseph. The eyes of the angel are fixed on the sleeping face of Joseph, who supports his head with his right hand; his left hand holds on to the corner of an open book. The whole scene is lit from one candle and the right arm of the angel protects us from its glare. When Joseph wakes up, he will, like Mary, give his assent to God's plan.

# Opening Response

In the name of the Father and of the Son and of the Holy Spirit.
**Amen.**

Joseph son of David, do not be afraid to take Mary home as your wife,
**because she has conceived what is in her by the Holy Spirit.**

# *Reading*

Matthew 1:18-24

This is how Jesus Christ came to be born. His mother Mary was betrothed to Joseph; but before they came to live together she was found to be with child through the Holy Spirit. Her husband Joseph, being a man of honour and wanting to spare her publicity, decided to divorce her informally. He had made up his mind to do this when the angel of the Lord appeared to him in a dream and said, "Joseph son of David, do not be afraid to take Mary home as your wife, because she has conceived what is in her by the Holy Spirit. She will give birth to a son and you must name him Jesus, because he is the one who is to save his people from their sins." Now all this took place to fulfil the words spoken by the Lord through the prophet:

> The virgin will conceive and give birth to a son
> and they will call him Immanuel,

a name which means "God-is-with-us". When Joseph woke up he did what the angel of the Lord had told him to do: he took his wife to his home.

# Reflection

We first meet Joseph when his life is interrupted by the aching discovery that his betrothed wife, Mary, is pregnant. What to do? How do you manage such an early disaster in a marriage and, as much as possible, save the face of all parties? Joseph's immediate resolve is to divorce Mary – a decision that is introduced by noting that Joseph is a just man, who would want to observe the Law, particularly with regard to sexual relations (see Deuteronomy 22:13-27; 24:1). He resolves not to take Mary to court to face a public inquiry before the rigour of the Law, but to divorce her quietly, in the presence of select witnesses, thus avoiding a public spectacle.

His life is interrupted for a second time, however, this time by the appearance of an angel in his dream who first counsels him not to be afraid, explains that Mary is pregnant through the power of the Holy Spirit and then goes on to challenge Joseph to take Mary home as his wife and name the child Jesus. What voice will Joseph listen to? Will he continue to listen to his own voice or will he listen to the voice of the angel announcing that God is doing new things, and that these new plans are counting on Joseph for his cooperation and blessing?

So this gentle dreamer must follow his dreams to plan the life of the Holy Family. He takes Mary home as his wife and recognises Jesus as his son. Jesus will be known as his son, the son of the carpenter. Joseph's life will continue to be interrupted – by the magi, by the command to flee to Egypt, by the command to leave Egypt and finally by the diversion north to Nazareth. Joseph responds to all these interruptions with generosity. We never hear of him again.

It's good to celebrate the generous people who are happy to live in the shadows, nourishing the greatness of others. Maybe we can think of our parents or grandparents, or others in our lives, people who were not hungry for the spotlight but were happy to play their supportive role, content that they were not key characters in the big drama of life. Jesus' life could not have progressed without these people. Neither could ours.

## *Prayer*

We bless God for the example of Joseph:
for his humility before the greatness of God's plans;
for his love and loyalty to Mary and Jesus;
for his willingness to change and adapt his life
so that the greatness of others might flourish.

We pray for ourselves that, in our turn,
we might be attentive listeners to God's word
and accomplish God's will in our lives.

May the Lord bless us through the course of our life
and accompany us in all our ways.
May he favour us with deep faith and hope,
that we might be alert not only to the God of yesterday,
but the God of today and tomorrow,
the one who is Alpha and Omega.
**Amen.**

## Closing Response

The virgin will conceive and give birth to a son
and they will call him Immanuel,
**a name which means "God-is-with-us".**

# THE EIGHTH STATION

## The Birth of Jesus

*Wilton Diptych,* **right-hand panel,** *c.* **1395**

The *Wilton Diptych* was painted by an unknown artist as a portable altarpiece for the private devotion of King Richard II, who ruled England from 1377 to 1399. The Madonna holds the Christ child, his right hand raised in blessing. The pennant bears the cross of St George, the symbol of England, and surmounting the staff there is an orb on which is a tiny map of England representing the country as the dowry of Mary. (For the left-hand panel see the Tenth Station.)

# Opening Response

In the name of the Father and of the Son and of the Holy Spirit.
**Amen.**

While they were there the time came for her to have her child,
**and she gave birth to a son, her first-born.**

# *Reading*

Luke 2:1-7

Now at this time Caesar Augustus issued a decree for a census of the whole world to be taken. This census – the first – took place while Quirinius was governor of Syria, and everyone went to his own town to be registered. So Joseph set out from the town of Nazareth in Galilee and travelled up to Judaea, to the town of David called Bethlehem, since he was of David's House and line, in order to be registered together with Mary, his betrothed, who was with child. While they were there the time came for her to have her child, and she gave birth to a son, her first-born. She wrapped him in swaddling clothes, and laid him in a manger because there was no room for them at the inn.

# Reflection

In the newborn Jesus the evangelist Luke gives us the icon of the living God, who enters history in the closing years of the reign of King Herod. In his story Luke registers the birth of Jesus as a child of a particular family, at a particular time in history and on a particular place on the map. The Gospel of John announces: "The Word was made flesh, he lived among us" (John 1:14) - there is no mention of a mother, a birth, witnesses, a place or a time.

Instead of proclamation, Luke tells a story: Jesus is not rootless, but is born a member of a specific family and tribe; he does not begin from zero, but enters an unfolding history between a yesterday and a tomorrow; he does not invent himself, but will discover himself as a unique link in a long line of faith. He is a Palestinian Jew born in the reign of Caesar Augustus and King Herod. He is in time and, therefore, in between times. In the person of Jesus God has visited the people. He has registered himself in place and in time. And that is what we celebrate at the birth of Jesus.

The birth story celebrates the newness of a child we honour as the Son of God. This is not hosanna in the highest but hosanna in the lowest - omnipotence in low profile. The focus is not on status and power but on littleness and vulnerability. While important adults appear in the telling of the story, like them our attention centres on the little one.

At Christmas we celebrate the love of God for us, which shows itself in the fragile bundle of the child Jesus. We celebrate our love of God through the person of Jesus. Perhaps it is true to say that we can love only what we can get our arms around. To love we need a particular name, a particular face, a particular person. And we have God's particulars in Jesus. When we look at Jesus we no longer have to guess at God: the best of what we know about God is revealed in Jesus. This little one is the one who shows us God. And, like Mary and Joseph, we can all get our arms around the child from Bethlehem.

## *Prayer*

May the joy of the angels,
the eagerness of the shepherds,
the perseverance of the wise men,
the love of Joseph and Mary,
be ours this Christmas.

Above all, we pray,
that the peace of the Christ child
and the gift of his peace
may be ours for ever.

And may the blessing of God almighty,
the Father, the Son, and the Holy Spirit,
rest upon us and remain with us always.
**Amen.**

## Closing Response

While they were there the time came for her to have her child,
**and she gave birth to a son, her first-born.**

# THE NINTH
# STATION

The Adoration of
the Shepherds

*The Madonna of the Pilgrims,* **Michelangelo Caravaggio, c. 1604**

Caravaggio transposes the adoration of the shepherds, ordinary folk, into his own time by presenting two ordinary pilgrims arriving at their destination and kneeling before Mary and Jesus. Standing on the doorstep of her house, Mary holds the child Jesus as she gazes at the two pilgrims. Christ's face is in shadow as his tiny right hand is raised in blessing. In this painting Mary and Jesus transcend both time and space: both of them can be reached by the poorest people.

# Opening Response

In the name of the Father and of the Son and of the Holy Spirit.
**Amen.**

Glory to God in the highest heaven.
**And peace to people who enjoy God's favour.**

# *Reading*

Luke 2:8-20

In the countryside close by there were shepherds who lived in the fields and took it in turns to watch their flocks during the night. The angel of the Lord appeared to them and the glory of the Lord shone round them. They were terrified, but the angel said, "Do not be afraid. Listen, I bring you news of great joy, a joy to be shared by the whole people. Today in the town of David a saviour has been born to you; he is Christ the Lord. And here is a sign for you: you will find a baby wrapped in swaddling clothes and lying in a manger." And suddenly with the angel there was a great throng of the heavenly host, praising God and singing:

"Glory to God in the highest heaven,
and peace to men who enjoy his favour".

Now when the angels had gone from them into heaven, the shepherds said to one another, "Let us go to Bethlehem and see this thing that has happened which the Lord has made known to us". So they hurried away and found Mary and Joseph, and the baby lying in a manger. When they saw the child they repeated what they had been told about him, and everyone who heard it was astonished at what the shepherds had to say. As for Mary, she treasured all these things and pondered them in her heart. And the shepherds went back glorifying and praising God for all they had heard and seen; it was exactly as they had been told.

# Reflection

One of the peculiar things about the two Gospel stories of Jesus' birth is that the account of the birth doesn't take up much space in the narrative. The birth is narrated in a half-line by Matthew: "she gave birth to a son; and he named him Jesus" (Matthew 1:25). Luke is fulsome by comparison, having two sentences: "While they were there, the time came for her to have a child, and she gave birth to a son, her first-born. She wrapped him in swaddling clothes, and laid him in a manger because there was no room for them at the inn" (Luke 2:6-7). Like the death of Jesus, the birth of Jesus is passed over in language that is surprisingly spare for such a momentous event. There are no details of this dramatic birth, no reactions noted from Mary or Joseph, no voices – not even a cry. Like the death of Jesus, the story of his birth is told through the eyes of the observers, those who come from near or far to witness the event.

The shepherds are Bethlehem locals, poor people, who are watching their flocks by night. They are graced with an angelic annunciation, surrounded by the glory of God, and treated to a bravura performance of five-part angelic choirs singing the Gloria.

It is as representatives of the little people, whose voice is of no account, that the despised shepherds make their way to the manger. They bring nothing with them. Often cribs show them bringing a gentle lamb or wild flowers or fruit, but this is not in the Gospel text. Unlike the wise men, it is not their gifts or their wisdom that they bring: they bring their poverty of spirit, their poverty of reputation, their poverty of character. They represent the kind of people that Jesus will have a special heart for in his later ministry, his ain folk.

They rejoice in finding one so close to their own poverty, one whose first resting place on earth is an emergency landing – what is available at the time – a borrowed feeding trough for animals. The shepherds can see that this child looks like one of them. They were told something amazing: that this child is born "to you". He is theirs.

# *Prayer*

O Lord Jesus Christ,
your first visitors were the shepherds
from the surrounding hills of David's town,
forerunners of the kind of people you especially loved.

We pray to you as our good shepherd
who seeks out the lost and calls us by name.
Have pity on those who have wandered far from you;
bind up those who are broken of heart;
strengthen those who are weak
and lead us all into the joy of your presence.
**Amen.**

# Closing Response

I bring you news of great joy,
a joy to be shared by the whole people.
**Today in the town of David a saviour has been born to you;
he is Christ the Lord.**

# THE TENTH
# STATION

# The Adoration
# of the Magi

*The Wilton Diptych,* **left-hand panel, c. 1395**

Three kings of England appear in this panel as they come to adore Jesus. Kneeling is King Richard II who is being presented to the Christ child by King Edmund the Martyr on the left and King Edward the Confessor in the middle, both venerated as saints: they both point to the kneeling king. Richard's patron saint is John the Baptist: he carries a lamb in his left hand and his right hand affirms the petitioner king. In the right-hand panel (see the Eighth Station) the Christ child welcomes the king.

# Opening Response

In the name of the Father and of the Son and of the Holy Spirit.
**Amen.**

Where is the infant king of the Jews?
**We saw his star as it rose and have come to do him homage.**

# *Reading*

Matthew 2:1-12

After Jesus had been born at Bethlehem in Judaea during the reign of King Herod, some wise men came to Jerusalem from the east. "Where is the infant king of the Jews?" they asked. "We saw his star as it rose and have come to do him homage." When King Herod heard this he was perturbed, and so was the whole of Jerusalem. He called together all the chief priests and the scribes of the people, and enquired of them where the Christ was to be born. "At Bethlehem in Judaea," they told him "for this is what the prophet wrote:

> And you, Bethlehem, in the land of Judah,
> you are by no means least among the leaders of Judah,
> for out of you will come a leader
> who will shepherd my people Israel".

Then Herod summoned the wise men to see him privately. He asked them the exact date on which the star had appeared, and sent them on to Bethlehem. "Go and find out all about the child," he said "and when you have found him, let me know, so that I too may go and do him homage." Having listened to what the king had to say, they set out. And there in front of them was the star they had seen rising; it went forward and halted over the place where the child was. The sight of the star filled them with delight, and going into the house they saw the child with his mother Mary, and falling to their knees they did him homage. Then, opening their treasures, they offered him gifts of gold and frankincense and myrrh. But they were warned in a dream not to go back to Herod, and returned to their own country by a different way.

# Reflection

As Luke concentrates on the visiting shepherds at the birth of Jesus, so Matthew concentrates on the visiting magi. The visitors have centre stage.

Matthew develops the scene with the care of a master storyteller. He ranges the wise men who follow natural means - a star - against the wise men of Judaea who are able to follow their own sign - the scriptures. It is clear from the story that the wise men of Judaea have enough information in the scriptures to discover the place where the new Davidic king will be born; but their discovery is useless, for it does not lead them to homage. They are not disposed to act on what has been revealed. By contrast, the pagan strangers, after they have gone as far as they can in following the star, are willing to be instructed in a scripture that is foreign to them. They act on what has been given to them, and their journey leads them to their destination. It is the Gentiles who follow the Jewish scriptures.

The wise strangers pass by the institution: their destination is not the exotic palace of the king but a child; their journey's end is not the institution of power but the person of Jesus.

The magi enter the marked house and, on seeing the child with his mother Mary, they wordlessly fall on their knees and do him homage. This child is their real destination, their determined focus, the object of their worship. They open their treasures now and offer their exotic gifts to this king. Whatever their plans were, a dream instructs them not to return to Herod and so become his accomplices: thus they return to their own country by a different way.

For Matthew, the wise strangers are the vanguard of all peoples who make their own journey to God in Christ. They may have taken a route that seemed curious to a religious establishment that had so many antique maps in their possession; but God draws all sorts of different people to him by all sorts of different routes. The wandering magi were led to God more by natural wonder than dogmatic instruction, and this has made them symbols of hope for all who struggle to God by strange routes.

## Prayer

To an open house in the evening
Home shall men come,
To an older place than Eden
And a taller town than Rome.
To the end of the way of the wandering star,
To things that cannot be and that are,
To the place where God was homeless
And all men are at home.

G.K. Chesterton,
from "The House of Christmas"[1]

## Closing Response

And you Bethlehem, in the land of Judah,
you are by no means least among the leaders of Judah,

**for out of you will come a leader
who will shepherd my people Israel.**

---

1    G.K. Chesterton, "The House of Christmas", in A. Thaxter Eaton (ed.),
     *Welcome Christmas! A garland of poems* (New York: The Viking Press, 1955).

# THE ELEVENTH STATION

# The Massacre of
# the Innocents

*Massacre of the Innocents,* **Léon Cogniet, 1824**

Cowering in the corner of a ruined building in Bethlehem, a desperate barefoot mother hides from Herod's soldiers intent on slaughtering her son. Most painters who have tackled this subject, like Rubens and Poussin, have painted a spreading spectacle of slaughter. Cogniet hints at this in the background but chooses to focus on the terror of one particular mother as she covers her child's mouth. She looks at us, the onlookers, as if begging us not to reveal her hiding place.

# Opening Response

In the name of the Father and of the Son and of the Holy Spirit.
**Amen.**

A voice was heard in Ramah.
**It was Rachel weeping for her children.**

# *Reading*

Matthew 2:16-18

Herod was furious when he realised that he had been outwitted by the wise men, and in Bethlehem and its surrounding district he had all the male children killed who were two years old or under, reckoning by the date he had been careful to ask the wise men. It was then that the words spoken through the prophet Jeremiah were fulfilled:

A voice was heard in Ramah,
sobbing and loudly lamenting:
it was Rachel weeping for her children,
refusing to be comforted
because they were no more.

# Reflection

Outwitted by the wise men, who have not returned to Herod as requested, the king orders the slaughter of all male children aged two years or younger. Although the massacre of the children is in keeping with Herod's character – he did not hesitate to execute anyone who threatened his throne – there is no independent witness to Matthew's story. It does, however, reflect the story of the birth of Moses:

- At the time of the birth of Moses, Pharaoh gives the order to slaughter every male Hebrew child (Exodus 1:22).

- Moses is kept safe as an infant by divine providence. Later he must flee his homeland because Pharaoh seeks to kill him (Exodus 2:1-15).

As the massacre of the children refers back to the persecution of the Israelites in Egypt by Pharaoh, so the reference to Rachel and Ramah refers back to the story of the Exile. Following the destruction of Jerusalem in 586 BC, Ramah served as a staging-post for Jewish groups being deported to Babylon. At Ramah the prophet Jeremiah witnessed the degrading exile of his people, inspiring his oracle quoted by Matthew, which associates the lamentation of the exiles with those of Rachel, whose tomb was nearby. Now Matthew associates Rachel with Bethlehem, an association that can be seen today in the shrine of Rachel's tomb, on the approach road to Bethlehem.

The death of Bethlehem's male children reminds Matthew of Jeremiah's prophecy. The matriarch Rachel is again weeping over her children; they are all her children, in every age and in every place, throughout time. She is the perpetual mother who refuses to stop grieving because the brutality continues over and over again.

Interestingly, the dominant image that Matthew chooses for this account is not the slaughter of the children but the matriarch Rachel weeping and lamenting at the loss of her children, stubbornly refusing to be comforted "because they were no more". This image is one that is simple and haunting and timeless. Rachel's grief symbolises that of so many mothers around the world today who live in the large absence of their children who have been taken from them. Their grief lies in an unfathomable place that consolation cannot reach.

# Prayer

O Lord Jesus Christ,
whose birth into this world
was followed by the slaughter
of innocent children in Bethlehem:
show your compassion on all who grieve
the violent loss of their children
in the midst of injustice in the world.

Tame the hands of all who visit
destruction and death on children,
those who care nothing for their innocence,
those who use them for their own purposes,
those who have no respect for the dignity of life.

Touch those mothers who are beyond consolation:
that their faith may hold fast
to what their hope cannot grasp.
**Amen.**

# Closing Response

Rachel wept for her children, refusing to be consoled.
**Because they were no more.**

# THE TWELFTH
# STATION

## The Flight
## into Egypt

*The Flight into Egypt 1,* **Gillian Lawson, 1979**

Home has become a dangerous place so the new family heads towards the territory of the old enemy, Egypt. Like all refugees, they are yearning for safety and acceptance; but it's as if the wind is protesting against the direction they are taking. The life of the great liberator Moses was saved in Egypt when his mother placed him in a basket. In this painting the frame of Mary's left arm forms a little basket of safety for the new liberator.

# Opening Response

In the name of the Father and of the Son and of the Holy Spirit.
**Amen.**

Get up, take the child and his mother with you,
and stay there until I tell you,
**because Herod intends to search for the child
and do away with him.**

## *Reading*

Matthew 2:13-15

After they had left, the angel of the Lord appeared to Joseph in a dream and said, "Get up, take the child and his mother with you, and escape into Egypt, and stay there until I tell you, because Herod intends to search for the child and do away with him". So Joseph got up and, taking the child and his mother with him, left that night for Egypt, where he stayed until Herod was dead. This was to fulfil what the Lord had spoken through the prophet:

I called my son out of Egypt.

# Reflection

From the exotic scene of gift-giving we move to a desperate scene of flight and murder. The family's escape is prompted by the appearance of an angel in Joseph's dream, warning him of Herod's intentions to kill the child, and commanding Joseph to flee to Egypt and stay there until he is alerted it is safe to return. Herod's power had no sway in Egypt, which had been under direct Roman control since 30 BC, and although the dominant memory of Egypt for the Israelites was as a place of bondage, it also served as a popular place of refuge.

In escaping to Egypt, Joseph is again seen to follow his dream, carrying out the angel's command. One of the characteristic elements in the story of the patriarchs is the frequent use of dreams in which they are called upon to face hardship and adversity that will challenge their capacity and commitment: four times Joseph is diverted through his dreams to take other roads. He would remind Matthew's readers of Joseph in the Old Testament, "the man of dreams" (Genesis 37:19) who went to Egypt to escape danger and later saved his family by bringing them to Egypt: again the image is of Egypt as a refuge. Jesus is seen symbolically to relive the Old Testament story not only of Joseph going to Egypt but also of Israel returning from there in the Exodus.

Matthew adds the editorial comment that this happened to fulfil what the Lord had spoken to the prophet: "I called my son out of Egypt." The quotation originally referred to God's calling Israel, God's son, from Egypt at the time of the Exodus. Matthew clearly sees Jesus recapitulating the experience of Israel: Jesus is the embodiment of the true Israel.

When your home place has become a threat and a danger, you have no option but to leave, becoming refugees, hungering for shelter and welcome elsewhere. If you are desperate for safety, you will not be fussy about the nationality or the colour, the religion or the language, of those who offer you welcome. All these things become suddenly irrelevant in the face of human desperation and yearning for human hospitality.

# Prayer

O God of love whose compassions fail not:
we bring before you the sufferings of all peoples;
the necessities of the homeless;
the plight of refugees;
the sighing of prisoners;
the pains of those sick and injured;
the sorrows of the bereaved;
the fragility of the aged and infirm;
the anxiety of all who are passing through
the valley of the shadows.

Almighty and merciful God,
you who are afflicted in the affliction of your people,
comfort and relieve all of them
according to their several needs and your great mercy;
for the sake of your Son and our saviour, Jesus Christ.
**Amen.**

After St Anselm

# Closing Response

This was to fulfil what the Lord had spoken through the prophet:
**I called my son out of Egypt.**

# THE THIRTEENTH STATION

# The Presentation
## in the Temple

*The Presentation in the Temple,* **Greek icon, anonymous**

Central to this icon is the ciborium, a covering supported by four columns that stands over the altar in a basilica. Mary hands over her son into the covered hands of Simeon, the prophet who has waited all his life to welcome this unique child. Behind Mary stands Anna, identifiable as a prophetess by the scroll she holds. Anna looks down at Joseph's offering – two turtle doves – which was the regular offering of poor people.

# Opening Response

In the name of the Father and of the Son and of the Holy Spirit.
**Amen.**

Now, Master, you can let your servant go in peace,
just as you promised;
**because my eyes have seen the salvation**
**which you have prepared for all the nations to see.**

# Reading

Luke 2:25-38

Now in Jerusalem there was a man named Simeon. He was an upright and devout man; he looked forward to Israel's comforting and the Holy Spirit rested on him. It had been revealed to him by the Holy Spirit that he would not see death until he had set eyes on the Christ of the Lord. Prompted by the Spirit he came to the Temple; and when the parents brought in the child Jesus to do for him what the Law required, he took him into his arms and blessed God; and he said:

"Now, Master, you can let your servant go in peace,
just as you promised;
because my eyes have seen the salvation
which you have prepared for all the nations to see,
a light to enlighten the pagans
and the glory of your people Israel".

As the child's father and mother stood there wondering at the things that were being said about him, Simeon blessed them and said to Mary his mother, "You see this child: he is destined for the fall and for the rising of many in Israel, destined to be a sign that is rejected – and a sword will pierce your own soul too – so that the secret thoughts of many may be laid bare".

79

There was a prophetess also, Anna the daughter of Phanuel, of the tribe of Asher. She was well on in years. Her days of girlhood over, she had been married for seven years before becoming a widow. She was now eighty-four years old and never left the Temple, serving God night and day with fasting and prayer. She came by just at that moment and began to praise God; and she spoke of the child to all who looked forward to the deliverance of Jerusalem.

# Reflection

The parents of Jesus take him to the Temple in Jerusalem, where they meet two waiting people, Simeon and Anna. As old people they are connected with the past of promise and with memory; Luke presents them as *anawim* – the devout remnant of those who wait on the ancient promise.

Simeon and Anna have spent their lives in longing to see the fulfilment of those promises. They are an unusual couple of old people because their total concern is for the future. They don't live backwards, but forwards. Something yet to happen draws their lives onwards. They are alive with expectation and hope, waiting for the one who will be the consolation of their own people and the light for the Gentiles. They do not live in the past; they are the opposite of the old people the poet Philip Larkin spoke of in his poem "The Old Fools":

> Perhaps being old is having lighted rooms
> Inside your head, and people in them, acting.
> People you know, yet can't quite name…
> 　　　　　　　　　　…That is where they live:
> Not here and now, but where all happened once.[1]

Simeon and Anna inhabit the here and now. So you watch Simeon take the child into his arms; you watch old age reach out for the flesh of a promise fulfilled, gathering this promise into his quieting arms. And you hear him break into the poetry of the Nunc Dimittis.

---

1　Philip Larkin, "The Old Fools", in *High Windows* (London: Faber & Faber, 1974), 19, 20.

And Anna: she is like some of the old women who seem always to be around our churches, praying and waiting, praying and waiting, and watching. Anna is always around the Temple night and day. She makes herself God's neighbourhood watch, and she has an energetic nose for what is happening in her neighbour's house. An inquisitive woman of faith, she is on permanent lookout: nothing is going to get past this old timepiece. Her timing is exquisite, since, Luke says, "She came by just at that moment" – she has been hanging around for years! This wonderful, attentive old woman now carries the story to all who have been waiting for the redemption of Jerusalem. The waiting is over; the Gospel begins.

## Prayer

Father of mercies and God of all comfort:
abide, we pray with all your people
as they face the evening of life.
Comfort them with the assurance of your presence;
grant them the grace of your abounding peace;
let your light shine on their path
and be with them until their days are over.

We pray also for all those people
who serve you in the person of the aged
and who devote themselves to their welfare.
May they always give their service
with love and devotion,
with patience and cheerfulness.
**Amen.**

## Closing Response

He will be a light to enlighten the pagans.
**And the glory of your people Israel.**

# THE FOURTEENTH STATION

## The Finding in the Temple

*Christ Amongst the Doctors,* **Giotto di Bondone, 1304–1306**

Dressed in a rich red robe and seated under the principal arch, the young Jesus is seen at home in the Temple discussing with the doctors of the law. As they listen it is difficult to guess from their expressionless faces how they find his teaching. Only one of them, the third from the left, is distracted by the arrival of their teacher's protesting parents. The parents are off-centre as they come to reclaim their child who will insist that he's not lost.

# Opening Response

In the name of the Father and of the Son and of the Holy Spirit.
**Amen.**

My child, why have you done this to us?
**See how worried your father and I have been, looking for you.**

# *Reading*

Luke 2:42-52

When he was twelve years old, they went up for the feast as usual. When they were on their way home after the feast, the boy Jesus stayed behind in Jerusalem without his parents knowing it. They assumed he was with the caravan, and it was only after a day's journey that they went to look for him among their relations and acquaintances. When they failed to find him they went back to Jerusalem looking for him everywhere.

Three days later, they found him in the Temple, sitting among the doctors, listening to them, and asking them questions; and all those who heard him were astounded at his intelligence and his replies. They were overcome when they saw him, and his mother said to him, "My child, why have you done this to us? See how worried your father and I have been, looking for you." "Why were you looking for me?" he replied "Did you not know that I must be busy with my Father's affairs?" But they did not understand what he meant.

He then went down with them and came to Nazareth and lived under their authority. His mother stored up all these things in her heart. And Jesus increased in wisdom, in stature, and in favour with God and men.

# Reflection

Like many Palestinian Jews, Mary and Joseph would go up to the holy city of Jerusalem every year, but this year is special because Jesus is now twelve years old. In later customs, the Jewish boy is introduced to adulthood when he is twelve - he becomes *bar mitzvah*, a son of the Law, assuming the responsibilities to which his parents had earlier committed him. In going to Jerusalem, it is possible that Jesus is celebrating an earlier form of this rite of passage: he is no longer a child; he has begun the process of being an adult.

The story tells us that Jesus makes his own decision to stay behind in Jerusalem without consulting his parents. On returning to Jerusalem, after three days, they find Jesus with the teachers in the Temple. He seems at home here, listening and answering questions, his insights provoking amazement. Previously, Luke has spoken of astonishment at what others have said of Jesus; now people are astonished at Jesus himself.

It also appears, however, that the sword that would pierce Mary's soul, prophesied earlier by Simeon, is already at work. Mary's question focuses on how troubled she and Joseph are: "See how worried your father and I have been, looking for you." Jesus' reply, however, focuses on his duty to his heavenly Father: "Did you not know that I must be busy with my Father's affairs?" Two different concerns bypass one another. The first words attributed to Jesus are spoken in the Temple and focus on his unique relationship with his Father: Jesus' first priority is to do as his Father commands him. His identity and direction in life transcend family history.

Luke says that the parents of Jesus did not understand Jesus' saying, a reaction to Jesus' words that will happen throughout his later ministry. Luke adds, however, the familiar note that Mary "stored up all these things in her heart".

Like all mothers do regarding their children, Mary will have much to store in her heart, not least what she does not understand about her son. As mothers have to let go of their child in the act of giving birth, so all mothers, including Mary, will have to let go of their child over and over again.

## *Prayer*

Lord Jesus,
we thank you for crowning our humanity
with the gift of a life lived for others.
We bless you for your struggle
to do your Father's will in all things,
even when it baffled and hurt
those who were closest to you.

Help us to hallow the Father's name
and be open to do the Father's will.
May we be steadfast in praying your prayer,
that our Father's will be done on earth
as it is in heaven.
**Amen.**

## Closing Response

Why were you looking for me?
**Did you not know that I must be busy with my Father's affairs?**